Bad Advice

The Most Unreliable Counsel Available
on Grammar, Usage, and Writing

John E. McIntyre

Apprentice
House Press
Loyola University Maryland

First Edition

Printed in the United States of America

ISBN Paperback: 978-1-62720-294-7
ISBN Ebook: 978-1-62720-295-4

Cover design by Kevin O'Malley
Author photo by David Hobby
Editorial development by Annabelle Finagin

Published by Apprentice House

Apprentice House
Loyola University Maryland
4501 N. Charles Street
Baltimore, MD 21210
410.617.5265 • 410.617.2198 (fax)
www.ApprenticeHouse.com
info@ApprenticeHouse.com

Critical Praise

"This is charming and smart (one of my favorite combinations) and, to be sure, extraordinarily useful."
  —Benjamin Dreyer, author of *Dreyer's English*

"A wise and helpful book."
  —Mignon Fogarty (Grammar Girl)

"The world of writing advice is riddled with bogus rules, misunderstanding, and pseudo-expertise. John McIntyre's concise and witty book sets the record straight using evidence, experience, and sound judgment."
  —Stan Carey, writer and blogger at Sentence first and Macmillan Dictionary Blog

"Grammar pedants confirm the adage that little knowledge is a dangerous thing. Happily for us, John McIntyre has a lot of knowledge about the English language and its uses. In *Bad Advice*, McIntyre excoriates the simplistic, outdated and just plain wrong "rules" that have long haunted English writing. Listen to him, rather than the ghosts of English teachers past, and your writing will be all the better for it."
  — Lynne Murphy, author of *The Prodigal Tongue*

"John McIntyre has written a guide that feels like a grammatical Innocence Project for guilty writers. This legendary copy editor takes a fresh look at the evidence presented by language purists and finds it wanting.

After reading him, I was moved to stare at myself in the bathroom mirror. Someone yelled, 'Not guilty!' It was me. Free at last."

— Roy Peter Clark, author of *Writing Tools: 50 Essential Strategies for Every Writer* and *The Glamour of Grammar*

For Kathleen,

*who, when I returned in excitement from the first national conference
of the American Copy Editors Society in 1997 to boast that the three
hundred of us present may have been the largest gathering of copy editors
in one place in all of human history, simply murmured,
"Except in Hell."*

Introduction

In Britain the monarch is never wrong. Whenever the sovereign drops a brick in public, a functionary turns up at Buckingham Palace to explain that Her/His Majesty "was badly advised."

In the same way, many of the things that you are getting wrong in writing are not your fault: you have been badly advised. You have been taught superstitions about English that have no foundation in the language. You have been hobbled with over-simplifications. You have been subjected to bizarre diktats from supposed authorities.

Much of it was well-intentioned. Grammarians of the seventeenth and eighteenth centuries lacking an established English grammar had to invent one. They turned to Latin, which had prestige and an established grammar they had been taught in schools, and they tried to adapt English to it. But Latin is a very different kind of language, and it was a bad fit.

Others have sought to tidy up the language by inventing and enforcing distinctions and prohibitions, seldom helpfully. (Look at the *over/more than* entry.)

We have wound up with what the linguist Arnold Zwicky has termed "zombie rules": absurd rules that have no foundation in the language and which have been repeatedly exploded by linguists and better-informed grammarians, but which roam classrooms and editorial offices like the undead.

As Henry Hitchings summed the situation up in *The Language Wars*, "The history of prescriptions about English ... is in part a history of bogus rules, superstitions, half-baked logic, groaningly unhelpful lists, baffling abstract statements, false classifications, contemptuous insiderism and educational malfeasance."

1

Likewise, advice on writing in general is marred by oversimplifications, half-heard advice, and idiosyncratic preferences—sometimes bizarre—passed off as professionalism.

Your teachers, editors, mentors, and supervisors have a lot to answer for.

And you have much to unlearn. Look inside and see.

I have kept the advice succinct. If you need further explanation on any point, look me up. If you want to argue with me, you can try.

Never end a sentence with a preposition

One of the oldest zombie rules, this is a classic example of shoe-horning English into Latin. In Latin, prepositions never follow the noun or pronoun they are paired with. The very word *preposition* means "place before."

So in the late seventeenth century John Dryden revised his work to eliminate what are now called "stranded prepositions," and his influence on the matter survives into this era.

But stranded prepositions are perfectly normal in English, and you need not strain to avoid them.

You can say, "What do you want this for?" and sound like a native English speaker.

Or you can say, "For what do you want this?" and sound like an utter prat.

Never begin a sentence with *and, but,* or *or.*

Conjunctions are supposed to link things, not stand apart, and there is some stylistic warrant for this "rule." A series of sentences beginning with *and* could make you sound like a giddy teenager.

But it is perfectly all right to use the coordinating conjunction *but* at the beginning of a sentence to emphasize the contrast with the previous statement. And it is perfectly all right to use *and* at the beginning of a sentence to emphasize the continuity with or amplification of the previous sentence. Or you could continue to observe a schoolroom oversimplification to which experienced writers pay no attention. (See?)

In the Authorized Version of the Bible, the first chapter of Genesis, describing the creation of the universe and humanity, has thirty-two sentences beginning with *and.* The repetition has a rhetorical power suggesting the continuedness and interconnectedness of the action.

"And God saw that it was good."

If it was good enough for Jehovah, it should be good enough for you.

Do not split infinitives.

Here we have another superstition rising from the mistaken belief that to be correct, English must be like Latin. In Latin, infinitives are single words and cannot be split. The thinking, if one wishes to call it that, is that the English infinitive, the preposition *to* plus a verb, must therefore be treated as a unit. Actually, as *Merriam-Webster's Dictionary of English Usage* points out, "The term is actually a misnomer, as *to* is only an appurtenance of the infinitive, which is the uninflected form of the verb."

Henry Watson Fowler, writing in *Modern English Usage* nearly a century ago (1926!), pointed out that fussing around with infinitives to avoid splits was highly likely to result in (a) awkward language or (b) outright ambiguity. But this peculiar superstition has got a hold on schoolrooms and editorial offices and *will not die.*

Bryan A. Garner, in *Garner's Modern English Usage*, quotes George Bernard Shaw: "There is a busybody on your staff who devotes a lot of his time to chasing split infinitives. Every good literary craftsman splits infinitives when the sense demands it. I call for the immediate dismissal of this pedant. It is of no consequence whether he decides to go quickly or quickly to go or to quickly go. The important thing is that he should go at once."

Raymond Chandler wrote a letter, now famous, to the editor of *The Atlantic Monthly* in which he complained about the editing of an article: "By the way, would you convey my compliments to the purist who reads your proofs and tell him or her that I write in a sort of broken-down patois which is something like the way a Swiss waiter talks, and that when I split an infinitive, God damn it, I split it so it will stay split."

Do not split an auxiliary verb from the main verb with an adverb.

Over the years, the split infinitive superstition, wrong in the first place, has been expanded into another area, the belief that compound verbs must not be split.

Eric Partridge in *Usage and Abusage* writes: "In a compound verb *(have seen)* with an adverb, the adverb comes between the auxiliary and the participle ("I have *never* seen her"); or, if there are two or more auxiliaries, immediately after the first auxiliary ("I have *always* been intending to go to Paris"); that order is changed only to obtain emphasis, as in "I never have seen her" (with stress on "have"). ... There is, however, a tendency to move the adverb from its rightful and natural position for inadequate reasons. ..."

The tendency Partridge alludes to has been prevalent among American journalists, the "split-verb" prohibition apparently having been invented by nineteenth-century American newspaper editors and propagated among their descendants and journalism school faculty. Journalists have been so schooled to write things like "we always have done it this way" that it sounds more natural to them than the idiomatic "we have always done it this way."

This nonsensical rule was kept on life support by *The Associated Press Stylebook* until 2019, when the stylebook editors were persuaded to drop it and announced the decision at the national conference of ACES: The Society for Editors.

Better late than never.

Do not use *none* as a plural.

Merriam-Webster's Dictionary of English Usage opens the *none* entry colorfully: "A specter is haunting English usage—the specter of the singular *none*. No one knows who set abroad the notion that *none* could only be a singular, but abroad it is. ... Mary Vaiana Taylor, in an article titled "The Folklore of Usage" in *American Speech* (April 1974), says that 60 percent of the graduate teaching assistants she surveyed marked *none* with a plural verb as wrong in students' papers."

While "none" can certainly mean "not one," the etymology that most of the singularists assume to be correct, the word can also mean "not any," and both senses have been current in the language since Old English.

The Old English *nan*, "none," "not one," was indeed a singular, as *MWDEU* points out. But it was inflected and had a plural form. Over the years, the singular form survived as *none* in both singular and plural uses, and you can use it as either, as context indicates.

That cannot be used to refer to human beings, only to animals or inanimate objects.

The *Associated Press Stylebook* distinction that *who* refers to people and named animals, *that* to inanimate objects and un-named animals is generally the case—but not universally so.

Garner's Modern American Usage says bluntly, "It's a silly fetish to say that *who* is the only relative pronoun that can refer to humans."

There are two major contexts in which *that* is an appropriate pronoun to refer to human beings.

The first is in references to groups of people, as in "The people that walked in darkness have seen a great light" (Isaiah 9:2 and Handel's *Messiah*). The second is in reference to a person whose identity is not known, as in "The girl that I marry will have to be / As soft and pink as a nursery" (Irving Berlin, *Annie Get Your Gun*).

You want to argue that *that* can never refer to human beings, you have the Authorized Version and Irving Berlin to contend with, and you're going to lose.

Always delete *that.*

There is weird hostility out there to an innocuous relative pronoun.

You can safely delete *that* when two short clauses are joined: "She said she was sick." No one will misunderstand or object.

But some editors and teachers go too far and delete the *thats* wholesale. Even the *Associated Press Stylebook* indicates a number of cases in which the relative pronoun is necessary:

Item: When a time element intervenes between the verb and the dependent clause: "She said Sunday that she was sick."

Item: When certain verbs are used: *advocate, asset, contend, declare, estimate, make clear, point out, propose,* and *state.*

Item: When the subordinate clause begins with *after, although, because, before, in addition to, until,* and *while.* "She said that after she ate the oysters she was sick."

Moreover, if you have two subordinate clauses, the second of which is introduced by *that,* you will do the reader and the cause of parallelism a favor by including the first one as well: "She said *that* she was sick and *that* she planned to see her doctor in the morning."

When *that* is there and does no harm, take your hands off the keyboard.

Always use *that* with restrictive clauses, *which* with nonrestrictive.

In the early twentieth century H.W. Fowler expressed a pious hope that English would be tidier if everyone adopted this distinction.

Relative clauses beginning with *that*, then, would always single out the one thing among the two or several available, and relative clauses beginning with *which* would always contain parenthetical material not essential to the sentence, set off with commas.

Those happy-go-lucky, carefree Brits have simply ignored Fowler's advice, merrily using *which* with both nonrestrictive and restrictive clauses and Bob's your uncle. But Americans have not merely taken the advice to heart; they have turned a suggestion into a Rule.

It is a Rule, among other places, in *The Elements of Style*. But the distinguished linguist Geoffrey Pullum points out in a post at Language Log, "That which doesn't apply to English," E.B. White altered the text of the book to "conceal the fact that his old mentor Willim Strunk know nothing of it and had never obeyed it. (Jan Freeman Discovered this.)"

The central Rule in English grammar is "Generally, with some exceptions." There are exceptions to the *that/which* distinction.

In a post at *Lingua Franca*, "A Rule Which Will Live in Infamy," Professor Pullum points out three significant exceptions to the *that/which* rule:

"The putative ban can't apply when a preposition precedes the relative pronoun: *the town in which she lived* is grammatical but *the town in that she lived* isn't.

"The supposed rule should be ignored when modifying demonstrative *that*, because *that which you prefer* is clearly preferable to *that that you prefer*.

"The rule can't apply to a conjoined *which*: *We must trust the unknown entity who or which created us* is grammatical but *We must trust the unknown entity who or that created us* isn't."

My comrades in the editing trenches have long fretted needlessly over this. You do not have to.

Do not use *they* as a singular.

Grammarians have long complained about a particular inadequacy in the English language, the lack of a gender-neutral third-person singular pronoun—a non-gender-specific pronoun to refer back to a non-gender-specific antecedent. Many people have struggled to invent pronouns to remedy the deficiency, none of which have gained traction. Dennis Baron, a linguist, has catalogued dozens of these inventions, all failures.

The remedy has been under speakers' noses the whole time: It is *they*.

The default masculine—always use *he, him,* or *his*—when the gender of the antecedent is unknown was an attempt by nineteenth- and twentieth-century grammarians to tidy up the language, but by the latter half of the twentieth century that usage had become intolerably sexist. That left writers with the clumsy *he* or *she* constructions.

Chaucer used *they* as a singular in the *Canterbury Tales*. Among the other reputable writers *Merriam-Webster's Dictionary of English Usage* cites as being given to the usage are Swift, Austen, Byron, Thackeray, Orwell, and Auden.

And oddly, those whose empurpled wattles tremble when a native speaker uses singular *they* themselves often use the singular *you* without a quiver.

Singular *they* is a non-sexist third-person gender-neutral singular sanctioned by more than six centuries of common use—older, in fact, than singular *you*. Even the *Chicago Manual of Style* and the *Associated Press Stylebook* have grudgingly come to accept it in limited circumstances. There is no valid reason to object to it further.

Now, brace yourself for the use of *themself*.

Do not begin a sentence with *however*.

Strunk and White's *Elements of Style* is one of many dated usage manuals that sternly uphold this guideline. These manuals insist that *however* can only be used as an interjection within a sentence, not at the beginning. However, Strunk and White is not the boss of you.

Garner's Modern English Usage says that the only objection to starting a sentence with *however*, in the sense of "but" or "nevertheless," is that it can sound ponderous. But that is a stylistic objection, not a point of grammar or standard usage. (And, mind you, how is *however* more ponderous than *nevertheless*, when it is one syllable shorter?)

Don't use *data* or *media* as singulars.

The English language treats other languages the way that speakers of British and American English have treated other people's land: It's there for the taking. It appropriates words for its own purposes and can be cavalier about pronunciation (Think what the French would say about the way we pronounce *lingerie*) or the original gender and number.

English has freely lifted from Latin, sometimes retaining the original gender and number, as in *alumnus, alumna, alumni, alumnae* (though *alum/alums* is gaining on them). But it doesn't have to, because it's English and it does what it pleases, thank you. *Datum* has largely fallen out of use except in technical documents, and *data* is now either plural, referring to all the elements, or singular, referring to the information as a mass.

If you want to make a political argument against *media* as a singular, on the grounds that each medium—newspaper, magazine, book publisher, online publisher, radio, television, movies—is distinct and should not be lumped into a monolithic group, go ahead. I've tried that, and no one pays any attention. English goes where it will.

Decimate can only mean to reduce by one-tenth.

That is in fact the original sense of the word, when it meant the Roman military custom of punishing mutineers by executing every tenth man, *pour encourager les autres* (though it originally referred more frequently to taxation than to military discipline).

The belief that the root *deci-*, the Latin for *ten*, should govern the meaning of the word is an example of what linguists call the etymological fallacy. It's instructive to know the original meaning of a word, but words are given to what linguists call semantic drift, changes in meaning. Look up the histories of *silly* and *nice* sometime to see just how far words can drift from their original moorings. (All right, I'll tell you. *Silly* has meant, over the centuries, *happy, pious, innocent, weak, pitiable, feeble-minded,* and *foolish. Nice* has variously meant *timid, fastidious, fussy, dainty, precise, agreeable, kind,* and *thoughtful.* You're welcome.)

Today, unless you are a centurion in a Roman legion, you will have little occasion to use *decimate* in its original sense, but its sense now includes "substantially damage" and "substantially reduce" in general and unexceptionable usage.

Don't use *over* to mean *more than*.

The keening among journalists when the editors of the *Associated Press Stylebook* announced in 2014 that they were dropping the *over/more than* distinction went on for weeks, and whimpering is occasionally audible to this day.

The imagined *over/more than* distinction, for those of you whose English usage was not corrupted by a journalism school, is this: *Over* must be limited to spatial relationships; it must not be used to indicate quantities. You can hold your hand *over* the baby's head, but you cannot say that the baby is *over a foot and a half tall.* You must say that the baby is *more than a foot and a half tall.*

This is nonsense. Lexicographers attending the national conference of the American Copy Editors Society at which this change was announced were floored; they had never observed any such distinction of meaning in the wild, and they had no idea that there were professional people following it.

Research indicates that the "rule" about *over/more than* was invented by American newspaper editors of the nineteenth century, among them William Cullen Bryant of the *New York Evening Post,* and propagated by subsequent generations of editors and journalism instructors.

The *over/more than* distinction is a classic illustration of Thoreau's observation that "any fool can make a rule and every fool will mind it."

Don't use *like* to mean *such as*.

I thought this piece of minor pedantry to be extinct, but it recently cropped up in a Twitter feed of advice on usage.

The thinking behind the distinction is that *like* indicates resemblances while *such as* indicates examples. You cannot say that "he is an orator like Winston Churchill," because Churchill is an example not a resemblance—provided you can discern a distinction that gossamer. You must say that "he is an orator such as Winston Churchill."

(Mind you, there is a further level of minor pedantry that bristles at the use of *such as* with a single example. Some people cannot be satisfied.)

To simplify your life, turn to the *like* entry in Merriam-Webster, where one of the senses listed is a conjunction meaning "such as," as indeed it has for lo, these many years.

Don't use *since* to mean *because.*

The imagined distinction here is that *since* must be limited to temporal contexts, reserving *because* for causal contexts.

You may have noticed that an English word can have more than one meaning, and *since* is one of those words, having both temporal and causal senses. Maintaining this distinction is as futile and time-wasting as the supposed *over/more than* distinction.

Always use *fewer* with number nouns, *less* with quantity nouns.

A reader chided me, gently, for the construction "one less item," suggesting that I should have written "one fewer item," to observe the count noun/mass noun distinction.

Yes, you will want to use *less* sugar in the recipe so that there will be *fewer* calories in the dish. And I understand that there are people left in emotional distress when they see a sign in a supermarket lane specifying "10 items or less."

But English always has more wrinkles in it than can be encompassed by a schoolroom maxim. *Merriam-Webster's Dictionary of English Usage* points out that Alfred the Great used *less* with countables in A.D. 888, and it has been common in English since, particularly in *less than* constructions.

Don't use *loan* as a verb.

English speakers and writers have used *loan* as a verb for centuries. But a popular usage commentator in the late nineteenth-century objected to it on etymological grounds on which he was flat wrong, but it got into all the schoolbooks, because textbooks copy previous textbooks rather than look into things. You can use *loan* as a verb without fear or shame.

Merriam-Webster does note that the verb is restricted to money or physical objects. You can loan five dollars or a lawn mower, but you use lend for figurative expressions, such as "lending a hand" or "lending an ear," a distinction that can be maintained because it is found in common usage.

Don't use *between* for more than two parties; use *among*.

Most of the time this is safe, but not always.

It is possible to use *between* for three or more parties when they are participating serially and severally. Here's an example: If the United States secretary of state travels to the Middle East for talks involving Egypt, Jordan, and Israel, then the talks are occurring *between* the four principals, though they are never all in the same room at the same time.

Don't use *convince* to mean *persuade*.

This distinction I learned early and labored long to uphold. From at least the 1950s, certain usage commentators frowned on *convince to*. They said that one *persuades* a person *to* do something but *convinces* a person *of* something.

And it seemed to me that there was a nuance of meaning to be recognized and maintained, that *convince* is a stronger word than *persuade*, because I can be *persuaded* to do something even if I am not *convinced* that it is right.

No one has been persuaded by either distinction; the two words, in the sense of "bring someone to a belief, a consent, or a course of action," are functionally interchangeable. The language has moved on, and it is pointless to struggle against the tide.

Don't use *collide* for a crash unless two or more objects are in motion.

This quibble is so ancient that you may never have heard of it, but at one time editors maintained, perhaps out of misunderstanding of etymology, that a *collision* could only occur when two or more objects were in motion. Two cars could collide, but a single car could not collide with a tree or a bollard.

This is nonsense, and sometimes, blessedly, nonsense fades away.

Don't use *careen* to mean *career*.

This one may not make any sense to you unless you have a very old usage manual or are a sailor.

The distinction is that *career* means to travel recklessly at high speed, "to hurtle"; *careen* means "to tip over to one side," as wooden ships were careened to make repairs on their hulls. If you are writing or editing for a British audience, be advised that *career* has survived there. But in U.S. English, *careen* can have either sense, or in the "hurtle" sense have an additional layer of meaning suggesting unsteady motion.

Don't use *hopefully* as a sentence adverb.

The peeververein, the self-appointed guardians of the language, always find much to complain about, but fashions change even in peeving.

For many years, particularly the 1940s and 1950s, the word *contact* as a verb was widely scorned. *Contacting* someone was business jargon, the way those people in advertising talked. (Complaints about individual words are never about the words themselves; they are complaints about the people who use them.) But as the means of getting in contact with people multiplied, the scorn wore off the word, and today no one complains about it any longer.

Similarly, because peevers gotta peeve, the adverb *hopefully* came under scorn when it was used in the sense "it is hoped that." The stickler insistence was that *hopefully* had to be limited to the sense of "in a hopeful manner." One of the peeververein insisted publicly that *hopefully* as a sentence adverb could not modify a whole clause because an adverb of emotion could not do that. (Sadly, he was mistaken.)

Unfortunately, though the *hopefully* objection has begun to fade as the *contact* objection did before it, it was included in a revised edition of Strunk and White's *Elements of Style*, and there it will remain in perpetuity, like a fossil turd in amber.

Only must always be placed next to the particular word in a sentence that it modifies.

This is a kind of parlor game for quibblers. Take a sentence that contains the word *only* and move it around to get different senses and emphases.

"He only wants to do the right thing."

"He wants only to do the right thing."

"He wants to do only the right thing."

"He wants to do the only right thing."

Jan Freeman, who wrote on language for years at *The Boston Globe*, repeatedly wrote to counter James J. Kilpatrick and other *only* fetishists. The word, despite what some quibblers would insist, is not out of place in the first sentence, because, as Geoffrey Pullum has written, "The word *only* is frequently positioned so that it attaches to the beginning of a larger constituent than its focus (and thus comes earlier), and that is often not just permissible but better."

Use a comma wherever you would pause in speaking.

Copy editors get tarred with the smear "comma jockeys" for supposedly being preoccupied with trivial matters, things that no one else cares about.

But copy editors are the people who understand that there are two kinds of commas and how to use them. The two kinds are the grammatically required and the discretionary, or, if you will, the syntactical and the rhetorical.

Let's take the required ones first.

Item: Commas are required when two independent clauses are separated by a coordinating conjunction (*and, but, or*): "John McIntyre has worked thirty-two years at *The Baltimore Sun*, and he oversaw the nighttime production of the printed editions." The comma is not required in an independent clause with a compound predicate: "John McIntyre worked at The Baltimore Sun and oversaw production of the nighttime printed editions."

(Journalists, oddly, almost always omit the comma in the first case and unnecessarily insert it in the second.)

Item: Commas are also generally required with introductory or concluding subordinate clauses: "When he came to The Sun in 1986, McIntyre started working on the copy desk." Or: "McIntyre worked on the copy desk at The Sun, where he edited print sections of the paper."

Item: Nonessential or nonrestrictive subordinate clauses in the middle of sentences, typically beginning with *which*, are set off with commas: "McIntyre edited staff copy, which came to the desk at irregular intervals, for the print editions." Essential or restrictive clauses within sentences, typically beginning with *that*, are not set off with commas: "The copy that comes to the desk at irregular intervals is intended for the print editions."

Item: Appositives, words or phrases that are not essential to the meaning of a sentence but provide additional information, are set off with commas. (You have just read one.) "McIntyre, a *Sun* content editor, has been with the paper for thirty-two years."

Item: The name of a state when running with the name of a city, and the year when running with a specific date, should be considered to be appositives set off with commas: "McIntyre, a native of Elizaville, Kentucky, came to The Sun on September 2, 1986, to work on the copy desk. (For those of you who can count, there was a one-year gap of employment in 2009-2010.)

Item: The comma separates the items in a simple series: "editing, proofing, and correcting." The final comma, known as the serial comma or the Oxford comma, is optional in some style guides. It must be used when necessary to avoid confusion—even The Associated Press Stylebook acknowledges that. It combines with semicolons in a complex series: "editing, the first step; proofing, the intermediate step; and correcting, the final step."

Item: There are others—the vocative commas in direct address ("Hi, John"), for one—but these are the main ones to watch for.

But the comma, as David Crystal describes in *Making a Point*, his history of punctuation, started out serving a function like the rests in musical notation, indicating the length of pauses in a text being read aloud.

To this day, the discretionary or rhetorical comma serves the same function, representing short pauses in the rhythms of spoken language. You will see it used, and will want to use it, in transcribing speech or mimicking conversational rhythms in prose (as in this sentence).

You will not want to overdo it.

Don't use *said.*

This is one commentator's advice*: Avoid speech tags—"he said," "she said"—but identify the speaker by action. Not " 'Is that your dog?' she asked," but "She pointed at the creature. 'Is that your dog?' "*

Sometimes the searcher for elegant variation cannot abide a plain, commonplace *said* but must substitute some other word. I once worked with an editor who had been a journalism major in whose work nothing was merely *said* but was always instead *divulged.*

Said is a beige word that does not call undue attention to itself and is therefore safe in virtually all contexts. Follow the advice in *The Old Editor Says*: "It is seldom, if ever, necessary to write that someone added, affirmed, announced, asseverated, averred, avouched, avowed, barked, blurted, burbled, chirped, chortled, chuckled, contended, declaimed, declared, disclosed, divulged, drawled, exclaimed, expatiated, explained, expounded, gasped, imparted, insisted, intoned, maintained, mumbled, murmured, muttered, noted, observed, opined, orated, professed, quipped, recounted, related, remarked, retorted, revealed, screeched, smiled, snapped, sniffed, sniveled, snorted, spluttered, stated, tittered, wheezed, whined, or whispered."

Do not write sentence fragments.

Wrong.

Though they are frowned on in the most formal writing, sentence fragments, judiciously employed in more conversational writing, can be an effective means of punctuating a thought.

Type two spaces after a period at the end of a sentence.

This is advice from high school typing class in a bygone era. This was conventional on typewriters because every character had the same value—what is called monotype. But current word-processing software uses proportional typesetting, so it is no longer necessary, or even advisable, to put two spaces after a period.

If you persist in doing that, your editor will have to run a macro to delete the extra spaces, and will likely mutter about you under their breath.

And if you should type a handful of spaces to indent instead of using the tab key, you will hear the grinding of your copy editor's teeth, and it is not a reassuring sound.

Omit needless words.

Perhaps the most famous piece of advice from Strunk and White's *Elements of Style*, this dictum leaves open the question: How does one decide which words are needless?

E.B. White, in his introduction, recalls how William Strunk Jr. preached the word to his class at Cornell: "When he delivered his oration on brevity to the class, he leaned forward over his desk, grasped his coat lapels in his hands, and, in a husky, conspiratorial voice, said, 'Rule Seventeen. Omit needless words! Omit needless words! Omit needless words!' "

I remember wondering at age eighteen whether his uttering the rule three times violated his own dictum.

Maxwell E. Perkins, the legendary editor at Scribner's, cut 60,000 words from Thomas Wolfe's *Look Homeward, Angel*. A few years ago, the University of South Carolina Press brought out *O Lost: A Story of the Buried Life*, an uncut version of Wolfe's novel. I will leave it to you to determine whether any of those 60,000 deleted words were needless; in my own hot-blooded youth, when I was a reading machine, I could not get through the *edited* text of *Look Homeward, Angel*.

Of course there are throat-clearing words and wordy phrases that can be dispensed with: *it is clear that, it is obvious that, it is noteworthy that, it is significant that, it is generally recognized that, it is important to remember that, it is interesting to note that, it is widely understood that, it seems that, notwithstanding the fact that.* There's a piece of advice attributed to Mark Twain—though there is no evidence that he actually said it—"Substitute 'damn' every time you're inclined to write 'very'; your editor will delete it and the writing will be just as it should be."

When I was a newspaper copy editor trying to get articles to fit the allotted space, I could usually pare an article by ten percent without any loss of meaning or impact, often in a way that the writer did not even notice.

But it remains with *omit needless words* that the words which are needed will vary by genre, author, subject, and other variables. E.B. White is spare, but you do not want to turn William Faulkner into E.B. White; neither would be comfortable.

Incidentally, if you have a misguided fondness or nostalgia for *The Elements of Style*, you owe it to yourself to have a look at the bracing denunciation of it by Geoffrey Pullum, "50 years of Stupid Grammar Advice," published in 2009 in *The Chronicle of Higher Education* and available as a pdf: http://www.lel. ed.ac.uk/~gpullum/50years.pdf.

Never use a long word where a short word will do.

George Orwell's advice above echoes Winston Churchill's maxim, "Short words are best, and old words when short are best of all." Thus his speech to the House of Commons on May 10, 1940, upon becoming prime minister in the midst of World War II: "I have nothing to offer but blood, toil, tears and sweat." Four pounding monosyllables, all old, concrete words.

The popularity of longer Latinate words favored by writers in the eighteenth and nineteenth centuries has been eclipsed in the twentieth and twenty-first centuries by a preference for the shorter, concrete Germanic words English inherited from Anglo-Saxon.

And yet.

Here is S.J. Perelman, seasick and writing resentfully of his healthy wife on board ship in the opening of "Swiss Family Perelman": "Her brazen effrontery, her heartless rejection of one who for twenty years had worshiped her this side idolatry and consecrated himself to indulging her merest caprice, sent a shudder through my frame. Coarse peasant whom I had rescued from a Ukrainian wheatfield, equipped with shoes, and ennobled with my name, she had rewarded me with the Judas kiss."

You think this would be better with shorter words?

Don't use semicolons.

You've likely seen Kurt Vonnegut quoted to this effect: "Do not use semicolons. They are transvestite hermaphrodites representing absolutely nothing. All they do is show you've been to college."

Tastes vary. Writing on "The History of Punctuation" (collected in *The Size of Thoughts*), Nicholson Baker is nostalgic about nineteenth-century prose in which the semicolon (along with the colon) was thought a little inadequate on its own, and so was combined with an em dash. "Everyone used dash-hybrids. They are in Dickens, Wilkie Collins, Charlotte Brontë, and George Meredith. They are on practically every page of Trollope. …"

But if you do not want to write in what will look like an antique style, you can at least remember this. In formal writing, there are two places in which you *must* use a semicolon, like it or not. The first is to separate all the items in a complex series, in which the separate items include words separated by commas. The second is to join two independent clauses without a conjunction; using a comma instead will give you a run-on sentence.

In informal writing, such as fiction, particularly fiction that presents dialogue, you can eschew semicolons and use run-on sentences to indicate the rhythms of spoken English with impunity.

Do not use adverbs.

Stephen King's preference is widely known: "I believe the road to hell is paved with adverbs, and I will shout it from the rooftops. To put it another way, they're like dandelions. If you have one in your lawn, it looks pretty and unique. If you fail to root it out, however, you find five the next day... fifty the day after that... and then, my brothers and sisters, your lawn is totally, completely, and profligately covered with dandelions."

No doubt the three adverbs in the final clause, *totally, completely, profligately*, are intended to illustrate the misuse, but while *totally* and *completely* duplicate each other, *profligately* has a different sense, one particularly appropriate to the way dandelions spread.

What the Shun Adverbs crowd usually means is that you should avoid using *very*.

But you can also avoid the kind of overwriting in which every verb or adjective is accompanied by a guardian adverb. You can see the hazard in the old Tom Swift series of books, in which each *said* is accompanied by an adverb (one of the genuine offenses of telling instead of showing). It gave rise to the game of Tom Swifties, in which an adverb is applied to *said* in a way that puns on the meaning of the sentence:

"I don't think that congressmen should be able to send so much mail at the taxpayers' expense," he said frankly.

"Why, you haven't prepared the corn for cooking," he said huskily.

"I'm afraid I have poison ivy," she commented rashly.

"That girl has the loosest morals in town," she remarked tartly.

"Why did Clare Boothe decide to marry that opinionated publisher?" she asked lucidly.

"You shouldn't have stopped by the woods on such a snowy evening," she observed frostily.

Adverbs indicate when, where, and how something is going on, and you need them for the first two categories. The *how* is the troublesome one, because it is there that you will most likely be telling the reader something rather than showing. Keep the ones that are useful.

Don't use the passive voice.

You have been told that the passive voice is a wicked, wicked thing, to be avoided at all times and in all places. Both Strunk and White and George Orwell in "Politics and the English Language" emphatically say that the passive voice should be shunned, and they have been echoed by countless commentators.

That is a load of codswallop.

While passive constructions can be used in a weasely avoidance of responsibility ("Mistakes were made"), there are times that you will want the focus of the passive voice: when the subject of the sentence is the object of the action rather than the actor, because whom it is done to is more important than who does it.

Take an instance: "The governor was arrested and charged with driving while intoxicated." That puts the emphasis on the governor. Who arrested him? Who arrests anybody but the police? It's safe to assume for the purposes of the sentence that the police arrested him, but the important point is that they arrested the *governor.*

This, however, is not the only kind of passive construction, as Geoffrey Pullum points out in his article "Fear and Loathing of the English Passive." http://www.lel.ed.ac.uk/~gpullum/passive_loathing.pdf (Professor Pullum has taken a snarky glee in pointing out the many unobserved passives in E.B. White's and Orwell's prose.) In his examples, "He was laughed at," "That said, however, Korea is Korea, not the Philippines," "The government had the case investigated by the police," and "I had my suit made by a tailor in Rome," all of them contain passive constructions that do not use a form of *to be*, and they do not necessarily conceal who performed an action.

Incompetent advice about the passive voice on the internet is as common as chiggers in the tall grass. You will discover that much of this advice comes from people who cannot accurately identify a passive construction.

Some, for example, deplore the "passive tense," though the passive voice is not a tense.

Some appear to imagine that any construction with an auxiliary verb is a passive. Pullum cites an objection to "Five girls have died," though it is not a passive clause but an intransitive one.

There is also a good deal of fretting about expletive constructions, sentences beginning with *there is, there are, it is, it was*. They are also called existential clauses. When you sing "There is balm in Gilead," the subject is *balm* and the verb is *is*. Expletive constructions can be objected to because they are rhetorically weak, but they are not passives.

You will also note a tendency to identify every use of a form of *to be* as a passive construction. Forms of *to be* often serve as auxiliary verbs in perfectly active sentences. In "He was watching reruns of *Law & Order* until dawn," *he* is the subject, *watching* the main verb, *was* an auxiliary, and *reruns* the object, a perfectly straightforward active construction.

You need not heed the advice of idiots.

Set yourself a schedule.

Anthony Trollope describes his work habits in his *Autobiography*: at the desk every day, 5:30 a.m.-8:30 a.m. He set himself to write two hundred fifty words every quarter-hour, and he kept his watch on his desk to check his pace. If he finished one work before 8:30, he began another.

Early in his career, John Cheever got up every morning, dressed himself in a suit, went downstairs to a windowless room in the basement of his apartment building, stripped to his underwear, and proceeded to write short stories. At the end of his workday, he dressed and went back upstairs.

But I knew of a professor of English, chairman of the department, who kept his manuscripts in his desk and worked on them at intervals during the day as time permitted. He published a handful of books by this method.

What worked for them might work for you. Or it might not. You have to discover your own rhythm, time of day, place, method—whatever is congenial. Dress as you prefer.

The only thing to remember is that if you just keep mooning about, you won't get much writing done.

A paragraph is five sentences

A fellow graduate teaching assistant at Syracuse once asked his freshman composition class, "What is a paragraph?" One eager hand shot up. "Five sentences."

The five-sentence paragraph is a template for the tyro in expository writing: one topic sentence, three sentences supporting the topic sentence, one concluding sentence restating or reinforcing the topic sentence.

One would like to think that no teacher would impose on the impressionable young so brain-dead an instruction as to construct *all* paragraphs in five sentences, though pedagogy has produced some strange offspring, but it seems likelier to be a residue of something misheard, misunderstood, or misremembered.

A paragraph contains as many sentences as it need to accomplish its purpose.

Do not write one-sentence paragraphs.

Did you read the concluding sentence of the previous entry?

Murder your darlings.

This piece of advice by Sir Arthur Quiller-Couch echoes something that James Boswell reports Samuel Johnson saying: "I would say to Robertson what an old tutor of a college said to one of his pupils: 'Read over your compositions, and where ever you meet with a passage which you think is particularly fine, strike it out.' "

Both pieces of advice are overstatements that you would be a fool to take literally and destroy everything you take pride in.

But, at the same time, we are not necessarily the best judges of our own productions. We need editors who can be trusted to tell us what works and what does not, who can stop us from making asses of ourselves in public.

Your editor is the friend who points out to you that you have a length of toilet paper stuck to the heel of your shoe just before you step to the dais at the awards banquet. It's embarrassing to have this pointed out, but it would be a greater embarrassment without the timely piece of advice from someone who has your best interests in mind.

Also, you are not always as funny or as eloquent as you think you are.

Write what you know

This must be why there are so many manuscripts in which the protagonist is a twenty-two-year-old who is having trouble writing a novel, in which the author's colleagues, friends, and relatives are recognizably limned as characters.

Flannery O'Connor remarked once that "anybody who has survived his childhood has enough information about life to last him the rest of his days. If you can't make something out of a little experience, you probably won't be able to make it out of a lot." I understand her to mean that anyone who has reached adulthood knows enough of longing, disappointment, fear, anger, and other strong emotions to be able to transfer them believably into the situations of imagined characters. That's where what you know is a help.

But if you're doing journalism or other expository prose, you start with what you know about your subject, which will not be enough, and you set yourself to learn as much as you can.

And if you happen to be writing period fiction, you will need to do research to get the details right, which includes determining the appropriate language for the time.

Show, don't tell

This is another "as far as it goes" adage.

Sure, don't write "He was always angry." Write "His foot would stamp and his throat would growl, his hair would twirl and his face would scowl, his eye would flash and his breast protrude, and this was his customary attitude." And soon you will find yourself on the quarterdeck of HMS Pinafore.

Piling up nouns, adjectives, and action verbs will only take you so far.

Showing rather than telling can lead to overwriting, piling up pointless details and accumulating clutter. You can write "She ended the conversation, closing the door firmly in his face, leaving him standing in the hallway." But if you simply write "She closed the door," it may have more impact.

Writing is more than constructing an assemblage of brand names and stage directions. You will need to explore and describe psychological states, and you will eventually have to come up with some exposition.

Write the way you talk

There is an element of value in this dictum. As prose in general has become more conversational over the past century, the stiff formality that used to obtain in journalism and general writing is no longer prized.

In fact, one piece of reliable advice is to read your prose aloud, which will often help you to identify awkward syntax, wordiness, or confusion.

But you will be required on many occasions to use voices other than your own, particularly in the formal occasions of the academic or technical paper, in legal matters, in memorandums. If writing the way you talk is what you were told in high school English class in place of application to the study of grammar and usage, it will not help you there. You will need to make up for your neglected schooling. *Merriam-Webster's Dictionary of English Usage* and *Garner's Modern American Usage* are available to help you close those gaps.

And if your area is fiction, you will have to be a ventriloquist for your characters. You, in short, will have to be like Sloppy in Dickens' *Our Mutual Friend*: "Sloppy is a beautiful reader of a newspaper. He do the police in different voices." Look at the voices that Eudora Welty presents at "Why I Live at the P.O." and "Where Is the Voice Coming From?" and think about how many voices you may need to assume.

Yes, you have an idiolect, your distinctive habits of vocabulary, grammar, and pronunciation, and yes, you have, through imitation of the writers you admire, developed distinctive patterns and preferences in your writing. But writers have to be ventriloquists, not only speaking in the language of the fictional characters they may create, but also in assuming the vocabulary, syntax, tone, and other elements of whatever nonfiction they are called upon to write. Your own voice is merely one of many you may need to speak.

Your editor will clean up your text for you.

Don't count on it.

The first thing to keep in mind is that you may not have an editor. Editing is time-consuming and expensive, so many publications and publishers have diminished or even eliminated the amount of editing they are prepared to offer.

Your own self-editing may be the most editing you get, so it's high time that you got better at it.

The second thing to keep in mind—should you actually wind up with an editor—is the kind of editing you are engaged with. Developmental editing, in which you and the editor are engaged in a prolonged collaboration? Line editing, in which your editor is bringing issues of focus, structure, organization, and tone to your attention, for you to deal with? Copy editing, a pass over your completed manuscript with attention to factual accuracy, grammar, usage, spelling, punctuation, and other such issues? Or proofreading, checking for typos, garble, and minor errors?

Each of these levels of editing will identify issues within your work and present different challenges, but it's going to be up to you to deal with them. You will still have to fix what is broken.

Also, mind you, spell-check is of limited use. It will flag typos and inconsistent spellings of proper names, but it will not flag the wrong word spelled correctly. You'll have to know your homonyms, and English is awash with them. And as for electronic grammar checks—no naming names here—a number of them have been identified as giving stunningly bad advice. Sorry.

Your editor will destroy your voice.

No one enjoys being edited. Your editor sees things about you, knows things about you. Your editor sees your mistakes and knows the weaknesses in your writing. And having another party point out those mistakes and weaknesses is embarrassing.

When you have produced a text, your very own production, you recall the circumstances of its conception, you carried it through a long gestation, and with sweat and pain you labored to bring it into the world. That text is your *child*. And here comes some damn editor who takes one look and says, "Um-UMPH, that is one ugly baby."

One response is to whinge about the insensitivity, the cloddishness, the sheer unthinking brutality of editors.

Yes, there are bad editors out there: unskilled and trying to operate beyond their abilities; high-handed editors who will re-cast your text as they themselves would have preferred to write it; rule-minded editors whose internalized, rigid stylebook will leave every text with a coat of battleship gray.

But in four decades as a working editor, my experience has been that, almost without exception, the best writers I've worked with have been most appreciative of an editor's attentions, and the writers most in need of editing have been the most resistant to it.

Let me say that again: The best writers are most appreciative of an editor's attentions, and the writers most in need of editing are the most resistant.

In fact, your editor will pay more minute attention to your work than anyone else who ever looks at it, and that includes your mother. Your editor will strive to understand your intent, the substance of what you are trying to say, the means by which you are saying it, and the ways that it might be said more effectively.

If you look at the published manuscript of *The Waste Land*, you will see that Ezra Pound slashed an entire page of it and dotted the rest with comments like (not *such as*) "too tum-pum." And Eliot dedicated the poem to him: "FOR EZRA POUND / IL MIGLIOR FABBRO," that is, "the greater craftsman." It is also Eliot who observed that while most editors are failed writers, "so are most writers."

Your editor should be pointing out to you what works and what doesn't. Pay attention.

It's easy to find writers who complain that, but for the ham-handed interference of editors, they would have contributed to an efflorescence of English literature unmatched since the England of the first Elizabeth. Don't join that chorus.

There is also the matter of Florence Foster Jenkins to consider: Is your voice one that people care to hear?

Note: All right, since you asked. Florence Foster Jenkins was a New York society woman who imagined herself a soprano and insisted on giving recitals despite her complete lack of musical ability, occasions that many in the audience found hilarious. In 1944 she was persuaded to give a recital at Carnegie Hall, to scathing reviews. A recording of her singing the second Queen of the Night's aria from Mozart's *Magic Flute* has to be heard to be believed.

Idiosyncratic and wacky

I invited readers of my blog, *You Don't Say*, at *The Baltimore Sun*, to contribute the dumbest advice they had been given about writing. These are some specimens.

Item: Someone once told me not to begin a sentence with a preposition. I replied: "On that, we will have to disagree."

Item: My Grade 7 English teacher "corrected" my plural possessive, saying the apostrophe should never go after the s. That was the first time I realized being a teacher was no guarantee of not being an idiot.

Item: Instructed in junior high that all papers containing the word "like" would be rejected. We did delight in coming up with workarounds such as "in the fashion of", "much in the way of", "in a similar mode to", etc.

Item: Get rid of all versions of the verb "to be."

Item: A friend was actually rapped over the knuckles for writing "between you and me." The teacher insisted it should be "between you and I."

Item: I was told that readers wouldn't read any word longer than eight letters or any sentence longer than 27 words.

Item: I had a coworker INSIST that you couldn't start a sentence with an abbreviation. We were writing about the military and so had to spell out "Lieutenant Colonel Smith" every time it began a sentence.

Item: A college student I tutored said their hs teacher taught them each paragraph in an essay had to have the exact same number of sentences.

Item: I had a class with several students from the same high school. They had been taught that a paragraph is eight sentences and to indent after every eighth sentence.

Item: My fourth grade English teacher for some reason made us use two adjectives for every noun in our stories. We had to decide what the two adjectives would be before we started writing.

Item: One of my elementary school teachers told us that one uses "person" for one human, "people" for more than one, and there is no word "persons."

Item: Never to use the words 'get', 'got', 'nice' and 'went' in writing. Our (otherwise outstanding) year 6/5th grade teacher actually wrote them on slips of paper, set fire to them and dropped the burning fragments in the waste paper bin.

About the author

John Early McIntyre grew up in Elizaville, Kentucky, escaped, and holds degrees in English from Michigan State University and Syracuse University. He has been a working editor for forty years, first on the copy desk at *The Cincinnati Enquirer* and for more than thirty years at *The Baltimore Sun*. He has taught editing at Loyola University Maryland since 1995 and served two terms as president of the American Copy Editors Society (ACES). Since 2005 he has maintained a blog, *You Don't Say*, at Baltimoresun.com, in which he writes about language, usage, journalism, and other subjects. He is also the author of *The Old Editor Says: Maxims for Writing and Editing*, published by Apprentice House at Loyola University Maryland.

Your text is safe in his hands.

Apprentice
House Press
Loyola University Maryland

Apprentice House is the country's only campus-based, student-staffed book publishing company. Directed by professors and industry professionals, it is a nonprofit activity of the Communication Department at Loyola University Maryland.

Using state-of-the-art technology and an experiential learning model of education, Apprentice House publishes books in untraditional ways. This dual responsibility as publishers and educators creates an unprecedented collaborative environment among faculty and students, while teaching tomorrow's editors, designers, and marketers.

Outside of class, progress on book projects is carried forth by the AH Book Publishing Club, a co-curricular campus organization supported by Loyola University Maryland's Office of Student Activities.

Eclectic and provocative, Apprentice House titles intend to entertain as well as spark dialogue on a variety of topics. Financial contributions to sustain the press's work are welcomed. Contributions are tax deductible to the fullest extent allowed by the IRS.

To learn more about Apprentice House books or to obtain submission guidelines, please visit www.apprenticehouse.com.

Apprentice House
Communication Department
Loyola University Maryland
4501 N. Charles Street
Baltimore, MD 21210
Ph: 410-617-5265 • Fax: 410-617-2198
info@apprenticehouse.com
www.apprenticehouse.com